Pub Quiz Book

Whatever you choose to do, make sure you remember the golden rule...

Enjoy the Quiz

Table Of Content

1- Which British queen gave her name to a type of sponge cake?
A. Anne
B. Mary
C. Victoria
D. Alexandra

2- Which of these is an annual race between Putney and Mortlake in London?
A. Egg and spoon race
B. Pancake race
C. Half marathon
D. Boat race

3- The pudding traditionally eaten with roast beef has the same name as which English county?
A. Lancashire
B. Yorkshire
C. Sussex
D. Devon

4- Where is the official residence of the British Prime Minister?
A. Downing Street
B. The Strand
C. Whitehall Place
D. Constitution Hill

5- In what part of the UK is haggis traditionally eaten?
A. Northern Ireland
B. Wales
C. England
D. Scotland

Answer

1- Victoria   2- boat race
3- Yorkshire
4- Downing Street   5- Scotland

1- Legend says that St. George, the patron saint of England, slew what type of creature?

A. Phoenix
B. Unicorn
C. Dragon
D. Lion

2- The vegetable leek is the emblem for which part of the UK?

A. Scotland
B. Northern Ireland
C. Wales
D. England

3- In which of these countries is "Pommy" (Pommie) a term used for the English?

A. India
B. France
C. USA
D. Australia

4- What would you do with a "toad-in-the-hole"?

A. Wear it
B. Eat it
C. Let it out
D. Sing it

5- According to legend the nursery rhyme "Ring a Ring a Roses" r "Ring Around the Rosy") relates to which 17th-century British disaster?

A. Great Plague
B. Great Famine
C. Fire of London
D. Viking invasion

Answer

**1- Dragon 2- Wales
3- Australia 4- Eat it
5- Great Plague**

1- In 2002 Liverpool Airport was renamed as a tribute to which member of the Beatles?

A. Ringo Starr
B. George Harrison
C. Paul McCartney
D. John Lennon

2- Wimbledon is famous for which type of annual sporting tournament?

A. Cricket
B. Tennis
C. Hockey
D. Net ball

3- A "Cockney" comes from which of these British cities?

A. Liverpool
B. Glasgow
C. Cardiff
D. London

4- The Channel Tunnel, linking the UK to the rest of Europe, runs between England and which country?

A. Netherlands
B. France
C. Belgium
D. Germany

5- Which of these statements is true about unmarked English mute swans

A. They are all black
B. They do not have webbed feet
C. They cannot fly
D. They are owned by the Queen

Answer

**1- John Lennon   2- Tennis
3- London   4- France
5- They are owned by the Queen**

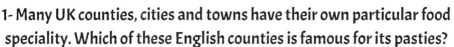

1- Many UK counties, cities and towns have their own particular food speciality. Which of these English counties is famous for its pasties?
A. Yorkshire
B. Cornwall
C. Sussex
D. Cumberland

2- The eisteddfod is a fine Welsh tradition. What type of event is an eisteddfod?
A. A festival of music and literature
B. A competitive sports meeting
C. A rally for steam powered vehicles
D. An agricultural show

- What is the name of the British born creator of the World Wide Web?
A. Christopher Cockerell
B. Clive Sinclair
C. James Dyson
D. Timothy Berners-Lee

4- Queen Elizabeth II is known around the world, but the royal family name is perhaps not so well known. What is Her Majesty's surname?
A. Wessex
B. Windsor
C. Westminster
D. Buckingham

5- The Giant's Causeway is a stunning natural rock formation. On the coast of which part of the UK is this wondrous sight located?
A. Northern Ireland
B. England
C. Scotland
D. Wales

Answer

1- Cornwall   2- "A"
3- Timothy Berners-Lee   4- Windsor
5- Northern Ireland

1- If you were to visit Scotland, you might enjoy a Highland Fling. But, just what is a Highland Fling?

A. An event at the Highland Games
B. A type of dance
C. An alcoholic drink
D. A romantic affair

2- The pantomime is a popular form of children's entertainment in the UK. At what time of year does this occur?

A. Spring
B. Autumn / Fall
C. Winter
D. Summer

3- Concorde is a beautiful aircraft, capable of flying at twice the speed of sound. With which European country did Britain develop and build this aeroplane?

A. France
B. Italy
C. Spain
D. Germany

4- Sassenach is the name given by one group of Brits to another. Which of these phrases describes the correct use of the term Sassenach?

A. Norse call the Scots Sassenachs
B. Scots call the English Sassenachs
C. Welsh call the English Sassenachs
D. English call the Welsh Sassenachs

5-A traditional dish coming from Wales is the Welsh Rarebit. Which of these phrases best describes a Welsh Rarebit?

A. Grilled cheese on toast
B. Chicken casserole
C. Oyster soup
D. Rabbit stew

Answer

**1- A type of dance   2- Winter
3- France   4- "B"
5- Grilled cheese on toast**

1- In which nation is "limey" a slang expression for a British person; especially a British sailor?

A. USA
B. Germany
C. France
D. Australia

2- Which Somerset village, famous for its gorge, gives its name to a type of cheese?

A. Stilton
B. Lymeswold
C. Cheddar
D. Wensleydale

3- Conkers is a popular playground game amongst schoolboys in the UK. Which of these are used to play the game of conkers?

A. Dice and counters
B. Cards
C. Coins
D. Horse chestnuts

4- On what date do we traditionally celebrate 'Bonfire Night' in the UK?

A. 5th September
B. 5th October
C. 5th November
D. 5th December

5- Which British seaside resort boasts a Royal Pavilion built in an Oriental style?

A. Portsmouth
B. Brighton
C. Blackpool
D. Southend

Answer

1- USA   2- Cheddar
3- Horse chestnuts   4- 5th November
5- Brighton

1- In which part of the UK was the industrialist and philanthropist Andrew Carnegie born?
A. Scotland
B. Wales
C. Northern Ireland
D. England

2- What are the main ingredients of the British dish known as 'bubble-and-squeak'?
A. Eggs and vegetables
B. Minced beef and beans
C. Potato, cabbage and other vegetables
D. Porridge and syrup

3- Which of these is a traditional English folk dance?
A. Morris dance
B. Fire dance
C. Sabre dance
D. River dance

4- What is stored in an oast house; a circular building with a conical roof?
A. Coal
B. Grain
C. Potatoes
D. Hops

5- Where was the English writer William Shakespeare born?
A. Stoke-on-Trent
B. Walton-on-Thames
C. Stockton-on-Tees
D. Stratford-upon-Avon

Answer

1- Scotland   2- "C"
3- Morris dance   4- Hops
5- Stratford-upon-Avon

1- Hogmanay would be celebrated in which of these UK cities?
A. Belfast
B. Edinburgh
C. Coventry
D. Swansea

2- What was Diana, Princess of Wales's surname (family name) prior to her marriage to Prince Charles?
A. Spicer
B. Simpson
C. Simmons
D. Spencer

3- On which day of the year are 'pancake races' traditionally held in the UK?
A. Shrove Tuesday
B. Ash Wednesday
C. Good Friday
D. Maundy Thursday

4- What family relationship does Queen Elizabeth II have with Prince Philip - other than by marriage?
A. Second cousin
B. Third cousin
C. Cousin
D. None of these

5- Margaret Thatcher was Britain's first female Prime Minister. Which political party did Margaret Thatcher lead?
A. Conservative
B. Liberal Democrat
C. British National Party
D. Labour

Answer

1- Edinburgh   2- Spencer
3- Shrove Tuesday   4- Third cousin
5- Conservative

1- Prior to 2015, if a person in the UK was given an ASBO what did they receive?

A. An honorary university degree
B. An order to behave in a civilised manner
C. A driving offence conviction
D. An order to behave in a civilised manner

2- Which King of England was killed when, according to legend, he was shot in the eye with an arrow at the Battle of Hastings?

A. Henry I
B. Harold II
C. Canute
D. Edward the Confessor

3- Bangers and Mash is a traditional British meal and can be found on many UK pub menus. What is Bangers and Mash?

A. Haggis and mashed turnips
B. Sausages and mashed potato
C. Prawns and mashed avocado
D. Meat pie and mashed peas

4- Scotland is the second largest country of the United Kingdom. What city is Scotland's capital?

A. Dundee
B. Glasgow
C. Edinburgh
D. Aberdeen

5- According to legend Saint Patrick is credited with banishing which creatures from the Irish mainland?

A. Rats
B. Unicorns
C. Snakes
D. Dragons

Answer

1- "D"   2- Harold II
3- Sausages and mashed potato   4- Edinburgh
5- Snakes

1- What is the currency of Gibraltar?
A. Euro
B. Peseta
C. Escudo
D. Pound sterling

2- Which English novelist wrote 'The Cruel Sea'?
A. Richard Adams
B. Charles Kingsley
C. Nicholas Monsarrat
D. William Golding

3- Who starred as 'Brother Cadfael' on UK television?
A. Sir Derek Jacobi
B. Michael Gambon
C. Anthony Andrews
D. Sir Alec Guiness

- The Robbie Williams video 'Supreme' featured which sport?
A. Motor Racing
B. Wrestling
C. Fishing
D. Football

5- Ringway is the old name for which airport?
A. Manchester International Airport
B. Heathrow Airport
C. Stansted
D. Prestwick

Answer

1- Pound sterling   2- Nicholas Monsarrat
3- Sir Derek Jacobi   4- Motor Racing
5- Manchester International Airport

UK History

Match them up with the decade:

1- Tower Bridge in London first opened to the public.

    A. 1860s
    B. 1870s
    C. 1880s
    D. 1890s

2- Notorious killer Jack the Ripper murdered his first victim.

    A. 1860s
    B. 1870s
    C. 1880s
    D. 1890s

3- William Lamb first became Prime Minister of England.

    A. 1830s
    B. 1840s
    C. 1850s
    D. 1860s

4- The Roman Catholic Relief Act completed the political process of Catholic Emancipation.

    A. 1810s
    B. 1820s
    C. 1830s
    D. 1840s

5- Jane Austen's "Sense and Sensibility", "Pride and Prejudice", "Mansfield Park" and "Emma" were all published.

    A. 1800s
    B. 1810s
    C. 1820s
    D. 1830s

Answer

1- 1890s (June 30, 1894)   2- 1880s (August 31st, 1888)
3- 1830s (1834)   4- 1820s (1829)
5- 1810s (1811, 1813, 1814 and 1815)

1- Victorian slums were notoriously dark, dangerous, overcrowded and often ill smelling places. Some of the older ones were given a nickname:

A. Rookeries
B. Slummies
C. Crime warrens
D. The Leytons

2- What was a cracksman?

A. Pickpocket
B. Mugger
C. Drug dealer
D. Burglar

3- In 1961, the inhabitants of which remote island were temporarily evacuated to the UK following a volcanic eruption?

A. South Georgia
B. Tristan da Cunha
C. Iceland
D. Barbados

4- James Hanratty was in the news in 1962, when he was accused of which crime?

A. Kidnap
B. Blackmail
C. Murder
D. Robbery

5- Which television channel made its first appearance on British screens in 1964?

A. Channel 4
B. BBC2
C. Channel 5
D. ITV

Answer

1- Rookeries   2- Burglar
3- Tristan da Cunha   4- Murder
5- BBC2

- In 1965, which of these people was honoured by a full state funeral?
A: Duke of Windsor
B: Lord Mountbatten
C: Queen Mary
D: Winston Churchill

2- September 1966 saw the official opening of a suspension bridge between England and Wales, across which river?
A: Dee
B: Tamar
C: Avon
D: Severn

- The Torrey Canyon was shipwrecked off the coast of Cornwall in 1967. What type of vessel was it?
A: Aircraft carrier
B: Liner
C: Supertanker
D: Ferry

4- In 1968, Enoch Powell made a speech which became known as the 'Rivers of Blood' speech. What was its subject?
A: Trades Unions
B: Immigration
C: Mods and Rockers
D: War

- 1969 saw the official investiture of Prince Charles as Prince of Wales at which Welsh castle?
A. Conwy
B. Caernarfon
C. Beaumaris
D. Pembroke

Answer
1- Winston Churchill   2- Severn
3- Supertanker   4- Immigration
5- Caernarfon

1- Dating back at least to Tudor times in England, and worn by young children, what was a slavering clout?

A. A bib
B. A terry toweling nappy
C. A rattle worn as a necklace
D. A miniature wedding dress

2- The first recorded official lottery in England was chartered by which expansive ruling monarch?

A. Queen Elizabeth I
B. Queen Elizabeth II
C. Queen Matilda
D. Queen Victoria

3- Medical practitioners in English medieval times believed that which form of the arts could heal various illnesses?

A. Painting
B. Dance
C. Music
D. Literature

4- England's Woburn Abbey, home of the Dukes of Bedford, also saw the birth of which very typical English tradition in the 1840s?

A. Tennis
B. Afternoon tea
C. Cricket
D. Skate board racing

5- Totnes in South Devon, England, is associated with Sir Francis Drake and which juicy fruit?

A. Plantains
B. Bananas
C. Coconuts
D. Oranges

Answer

1- A bib   2- Queen Elizabeth I
3- Music   4- Afternoon tea
5- Oranges

1- What charges led to the beheading of Henry VIII's second wife, Anne Boleyn?
A: Incest with her brother
B: Treason
C: Adultery with five men
D: All three reasons

2- 1981 saw the founding of a new political party in the UK. Which of these was it?
A: Plaid Cymru
B: Monster Raving Loony Party
C: Social Democratic Party
D: Green Party

3- Britain was at its military height during the 19th century. Which of these battles did NOT take place in the 1800s?
A: Culloden
B: Trafalgar
C: Waterloo
D: Balaclava

4- 1658 saw the death of which of these leaders?
A: James I
B: Charles I
C: Charles II
D: Oliver Cromwell

5- In 1476, William Caxton was the first man to do what?
A. Invent the parachute
B. Create an oil painting
C. Establish a whisky distillery
D. Establish a printing press in England

Answer
1- All three reasons   2- Social Democratic Party
3- Culloden   4- Oliver Cromwell
5- Establish a printing press in England

1- Which of the following events did NOT occur during the Regency period (1811-1820)?

A. The French Revolution
B. The Peterloo Massacre
C. The restoration of Louis XVIII of France
D. The publication of "Frankenstein" by Mary Shelley

2- While Queen Victoria was monarch for most of the nineteenth century, she wasn't there at the beginning. Who was on the throne when the 1800s began?

A. Anne
B. William IV
C. George IV
D. George III

3- The Battle of Waterloo took place in 1815 with the commanders being the Duke of Wellington and Napoleon. Who was Napoleon's second in command

A. Auguste de Marmont
B. Michel Ney
C. Jean-Baptiste Bernadotte
D. Ferdinand Foch

4- In 1822 Charles Babbage reported his construction of an automated mechanical calculator. What did he name it?

A. Mathematical mechanism
B. Calculating machine
C. Addition instrument
D. Difference engine

5- Which famous Northern steeplechase for horses is widely accepted as having been held for the first time in 1839?

A: St Leger
B: Grand National
C: Cheltenham Gold Cup
D: Derby

Answer

1- The French Revolution   2- George III
3- Michel Ney   4- Difference engine
5- Grand National

1- In 1842 which peace treaty was signed, bringing an end to the first Opium War between the UK and China?

A: Boxer Protocol
B: Treaty of Canton
C: Treaty of Nanking/Nanjing
D: Treaty of Shanghai

2- Prince Albert's brainchild, the Great Exhibition, was held in 1851. What was the name of the structure built specially to house the displays?

A: Glass Menagerie
B: Great Pagoda
C: Crystal Palace
D: Marble Arch

3- Which man became Prime Minister of the UK in 1868, the first of his several spells in this position?

A: Benjamin Disraeli
B: David Lloyd George
C: William Gladstone
D: Stanley Baldwin

4- Giles Gilbert Scott was born in 1880 and went on to make his name in which of these areas?

A: Films
B: Sport
C: Music
D: Architecture

5- An iconic British tower opened to the public in 1894 in which English town

A: Stirling
B: Blackpool
C: Portsmouth
D: Glastonbury

Answer

1- Treaty of Nanking/Nanjing   2- Crystal Palace
3- William Gladstone   4- Architecture
5- Blackpool

1- Mary was called 'Bloody Mary' because she burned a lot of heretics. Where did most of the burnings take place?
A. Glasgow
B. Bishop's Gate
C. Oxford
D. Smithfield

2- Who dealt with the political split with Rome during Henry VIII's reign after Wolsey died?
A. Cromwell
B. Buckingham
C. Dudley
D. Cranmer

3- What did the 1533 Act of Restraint of Appeals do?
A. Declared Mary I a bastard
B. Made Henry VIII pope
C. Made religious questions solved in England, not Rome
D. Made all religious questions go directly to Rome

4- Who talked Edward VI into changing the order of succession?
A. Buckingham
B. Northumberland
C. Mary
D. Cranmer

5- What language was Elizabeth I NOT fluent in?
A: German
B: Italian
C: Latin
D: French

Answer

1- Smithfield   2- Cromwell
3- "C"   4- Northumberland
5- German

1- Who was the English King who was killed by 'the little gentleman in the black velvet'?
A. George I
B. George II
C. William III
D. William IV

2- Of which of these did Edward VIII become the Governor after he abdicated from the British throne?
A. The Bahamas
B. Rhodesia
C. Isle of Man
D. Canada

3- Which famous Englishman was killed by a musket-ball fired from aboard the French ship "Redoutable" on 21st of October 1805?
A. The Duke of Wellington
B. The architect Nicholas Hawksmoor
C. Lord Nelson
D. William Pitt the Elder, Earl of Chatham

4- What happened on 8th August 1963 that shocked public opinion in Britain?
A. Sudden withdrawal of Harold Wilson from job as Prime Minister
B. Start of the Profumo Affair
C. Death of Brian Jones
D. Great Train Robbery

5- Which of these plots led to the execution of Mary Queen of Scots?
A: Babington Plot
B: Piltdown Plot
C: Plug Plot
D: Gunpowder Plot

Answer

1- William III   2- The Bahamas
3- Lord Nelson   4- Great Train Robbery
5- Babington Plot

1- Which of these ancient medieval castles was and, still is, the largest ever built in Britain?

A. Stirling
B. Caerphilly
C. Windsor
D. Warwick

2- How did the London baker Thomas Farriner aka Thomas Farynor aka Thomas Faynor get into the history books in 1666?

A. By inventing the recipe for scones
B. By causing the Great Fire
C. By surviving three attempts to hang him at the gallows
D. By being the first Englishman to swim across the Channel

3- Which of these palaces was Queen Victoria's Palace on the Isle of Wight?

A. Chequers
B. Balmoral
C. Sandringham
D. Osborne House

4- Which part of the British Isles was once ruled by the Kings of Alba?

A. Scotland
B. The Isle of Wight
C. Ireland
D. England

5- Which of these historic characters once had to hide in an oak tree to save his life after a military defeat?

A: Charles I
B: Charles II
C: Henry VII
D: Sir Winston Churchill

Answer

**1- Windsor 2- By causing the Great Fire
3- Osborne House 4- Scotland
5- Charles II**

1-True or false?
London was over the past called Londinium,
Lundenwic, and Ludenberg.

A. True

B. False

2- True or false?
England was part of the shortest war in history,
they fought Zanzibar in 1896 who surrendered after 38 hours.

A. True

B. False

3- True or false?
Buckingham Palace has its own police station.

A. True

B. False

4- True or false?
The Queen of the UK are the legal owner of one-sixth
of the Earth's land surface.

A. True

B. False

5- True or false?
The King of Norway is 73rd in line to the British throne.

A. True

B. False

Answer
1- True   2- False (after 38 minutes)
3- True   4- True
5- True

UK Geography

Reading the clues should help:

1- Eas a' Chual Aluinn is the highest of its kind in the United Kingdom.
A. Waterfall
B. Beach
C. Mountain
D. Forest

2- Carrickfergus protected much of Northern Ireland long after the Normans invaded.
A. Cave
B. Castle
C. Lake
D. Volcano

3- "Didn't we have a lovely time the day we went to Bangor."
A. Beach
B. Restaurant
C. City
D. Street

4- Fingal is asking for help to produce the eerie sound of echoing waves.
A. Landscape
B. Cave
C. Valley
D. Park

5- Bann is the longest of its kind in Northern Ireland.
A: Sea
B: River
C: Ocean
D: Gorge

Answer

1- Waterfall   2- Castle
3- City   4- Cave
5- River

1- "Not all that long ago, when children were even smaller, and people had especially hairy knees, there lived an old man of Lochnagar."

A. Desert
B. Mountain
C. Lake
D. River

2- Travel slowly across the Pontcysyllte Aqueduct to the nearby town of Llangollen.

A. Waterway
B. Canal
C. Bay
D. Ocean

3- Tresco is a very silly name and not at all like St Mary's or St Martin's.

A. Island
B. City
C. Valley
D. Oasis

4- Let us visit Beamish and take a tram into the not so distant past.

A. Cinema
B. Store
C. Museum
D. Supermarket

5- Coniston is longer than Buttermere and Wastwater put together.

A: Ocean
B: Dune
C: Landscape
D: Lake

Answer

1- Mountain   **2-** Canal
3- Island   **4-** Museum
5- Lake

1- Can you name this famous university city situated on the River Thames?
A. Calfcrossing
B. Yakarch
C. Cowbridge
D. Oxford

2- You need to identify this large town in Shropshire, situated on the River Severn.
A. Ratcliffe
B. Molehill
C. Shrewsbury
D. Volerise

3- Leighton ___ ; which bird completes this Bedfordshire town's name?
A. Hawk
B. Buzzard
C. Eagle
D. Mallard

4- Which area around Cardiff's docklands was formerly named after an animal?
A. Tiger Bay
B. Cougar Cove
C. Leopard Beach
D. Lion Sands

5- A few miles north of Dover on the Kent coast lies which town?
A: Wethersporch
B: Ramsgate
C: Sheepslock
D: Ewesdoor

Answer

1- Oxford   2- Shrewsbury
3- Buzzard   4- Tiger Bay
5- Ramsgate

1- There is a seaside resort in Dorset which has one of these 'fowl' names

A. Gooseage

B. Henage

C. Swanage

D. Duckage

2- Can you spot the correct name of a Staffordshire village from this peculiar bunch?

A. Sutton-under-Snake

B. Norton-under-Newt

C. Easton-under-Tortoise

D. Weston-under-Lizard

3- Which of these names is not a real English place-name?

A. Partridge Green

B. Woodpecker Green

C. Goose Green

D. Sparrows Green

4- Scotland now; which of these is an actual town?

A. Horsedenbeath

B. Bulldenbeath

C. Cowdenbeath

D. Plateofbeef

5- A small cove in Cornwall has which unusual name?

A: Mousehole

B: Foxhole

C: Molehole

D: Rathole

Answer

1- Swanage   2- Weston-under-Lizard
3- Woodpecker Green   4- Cowdenbeath
5- Mousehole

1- University town in Middlesex, with ties to the English Civil War and the Battle of Britain.

A. Hayes

B. Harrow

C. Slough

D. Uxbridge

2- Second largest of its type in the Lake District.

A. Aira Force

B. Ullswater

C. Derwentwater

D. Windermere

3- Traditional Irish province, two thirds of which is part of the UK.

A. Donegal

B. Belfast

C. Londonderry

D. Ulster

4- Town in Wales, Brynbuga in Welsh.

A. Monmouth

B. Usk

C. Abergavenny

D. Chepstow

5- Village in Gloucestershire that counts itself doubly fortunate.

A. Upper Slaughter

B. Bibury

C. Castle Combe

D. Painswick

Answer

1- Uxbridge 2- Ullswater

3- Ulster 4- Usk

5- Upper Slaughter

1- Group of islands in Scotland's Outer Hebrides.
A. Uist
B. Benbecula
C. Harris
D. Barra

2- Market town in Staffordshire, near Stoke-on-Trent.
A. Nottingham
B. Doncaster
C. Lichfield
D. Uttoxeter

3- Gloucestershire village noted for church with Tudor era timbered tower
A. Ledbury
B. Upleadon
C. Bromyard
D. Holme Lacy

4- Town in East Sussex, situated on a tributary of the River Ouse.
A. Uckfield
B. Lewes
C. Eastbourne
D. Hailsham

5- Village in Oxfordshire with a White Horse on a hillside.
A: Kelmscott
B: Uffington
C: Burford
D: Kingham

Answer

1- Uist   2- Uttoxeter
3- Upleadon   4- Uckfield
5- Uffington

1- Which Roman Emperor built a wall across Britain?

A. Augustus

B. Tiberius

C. Hadrian

D. Claudius

2- In which country of the United Kingdom is the amazing graphical feature known as the Giant's Causeway to be found?

A. England

B. Wales

C. Scotland

D. Northern Ireland

3- Where is the highest mountain in the United Kingdom?

A. Northern Ireland

B. Scotland

C. England

D. Wales

4- Charles, the Prince of Wales, is also the duke of which county?

A. Devon

B. Yorkshire

C. Gloucester

D. Cornwall

5- Where would you find the British National Gallery?

A: Trafalgar Square

B: Tavistock Square

C: Leicester Square

D: Portland Place

Answer

1- Hadrian   2- Northern Ireland

3- Scotland   4- Cornwall

5- Trafalgar Square

1- Which county was the home of the famous folk hero Robin Hood?
A. Norfolk
B. Nottingham
C. Lincolnshire
D. Derbyshire

2- In which country would you find the famous Portmeirion Village?
A. England
B. Northern Ireland
C. Wales
D. Scotland

3- At which racecourse is the 'Grand National' held?
A. Doncaster
B. Ascot
C. Windsor
D. Aintree

4- The citizens of which English city are often referred to as Scousers?
A. Gloucester
B. Preston
C. Exeter
D. Liverpool

5- In which country of the United Kingdom would you be able to visit Carrickfergus Castle?
A: England
B: Northern Ireland
C: Wales
D: Scotland

Answer

1- Nottingham   2- Wales
3- Aintree   4- Liverpool
5- Northern Ireland

1- Where would you find the Millennium Wheel?
A. Glasgow
B. Manchester
C. Liverpool
D. London

2- Most people have heard of the Loch Ness monster, but at which Scottish town/city does Loch Ness join the North Sea?
A. Inverness
B. Dundee
C. Stirling
D. Aberdeen

3- Which city have recent 2004/5 statistics shown to be the safest city in the UK?
A. Leeds
B. Belfast
C. Portsmouth
D. Sheffield

4- In which city is Old Trafford?
A. Liverpool
B. Edinburgh
C. Manchester
D. Newcastle

5- Where is the William Wallace monument?
A: Aberdeen
B: Stirling
C: Carlisle
D: York

Answer

1- London   2- Inverness
3- Sheffield   4- Manchester
5- Stirling

1- Near which city would you find Spaghetti Junction?
A. Stafford
B. London
C. Birmingham
D. Newcastle

2- Where is Cleopatra's needle?
A. Sheffield
B. Liverpool
C. Southampton
D. London

3- Which city is associated with the Mersey Ferries?
A. Newcastle
B. Liverpool
C. Leeds
D. Bristol

4- The rowing teams of which two UK universities hold a famous traditional annual race?
A. Oxford & Cambridge
B. Cambridge & King's College
C. Durham & King's College
D. Durham & York

5- Where in London is the Christmas tree displayed that is given to the City of London every year by the Norwegians?
A: Buckingham Palace
B: Oxford Street
C: Trafalgar Square
D: Piccadilly Circus

Answer
1- Birmingham   2- London
3- Liverpool   4- Oxford & Cambridge
5- Trafalgar Square

1- In which royal residence does the British Queen spend the months of August and September every year?

A. Windsor Castle
B. Buckingham Palace
C. Edinburgh Castle
D. Balmoral Castle

2- What is the national emblem flower of Scotland?

A. Shamrock
B. Bracken
C. Rose
D. Thistle

3- Where in Scotland can you find Arthur's Seat?

A. Stirling
B. Edinburgh
C. Perth
D. Glasgow

4- A famous London landmark is featured on an album cover of the British band Pink Floyd. What is the name of it?

A. Battersea Power Station
B. Tower of London
C. Houses of Parliament
D. Buckingham Palace

5- Which English county is the famous seaside resort of Blackpool in?

A: Yorkshire
B: Lancashire
C: Kent
D: Cheshire

Answer

1- Balmoral Castle   2- Thistle
3- Edinburgh   4- Battersea Power Station
5- Lancashire

Science
" British Discoveries'

1- While working at the University of Cambridge's Cavendish Laboratory, Francis Crick and James Watson discovered the structure of DNA took what form?

A. Sphere
B. Cone
C. Double helix
D. Figure of eight

2- What was the title of the 1859 work by Charles Darwin in which he set out his theory of evolution by natural selection?

A. Notes from the Galapagos Islands
B. On the Origin of Species
C. Survival of the Fittest
D. Descent of Man

3- How was penicillin first discovered?

A. Dr Louis Pasteur
B. Dr Ernst Chain
C. Dr Alexander Fleming
D. Dr Howard Florey

4- Which unit of temperature is named after the British scientist who discovered the value of absolute zero, the coldest temperature possible?

A. Fahrenheit
B. Celsius
C. Chilly
D. Kelvin

5- Sir Tim Berners-Lee is a British scientist who invented what when he made a hypertext transfer protocol communication using the internet?

A: World Wide Web
B: Wifi
C: Skype
D: Email

Answer

1- Double helix   2- On the Origin of Species
3- Dr Alexander Fleming   4- Kelvin
5- World Wide Web

1- Which scientist is known for his "law of universal gravitation" and his three "laws of motion"?

A. Robert Boyle
B. Francis Bacon
C. Michael Faraday
D. Sir Isaac Newton

2- James Watt is the inventor of the steam engine. However his engine was actually an improved version of the 'atmospheric engine' invented in 1712 by which British inventor?

A. Matthew Boulton
B. Thomas Newcomen
C. Robert Stephenson
D. Richard Trevithick

3- While working at the University of Manchester Ernest Rutherford conducted the 'gold foil experiment' which led to him forming a new theory relating to what?

A. The structure of atoms
B. The Higgs-boson particle
C. How metal conducts electricity
D. The concept of the radioactive half-life

4- Edward Jenner created the first vaccine in 1796 after noticing that milkmaids who had caught the less virulent cowpox were granted immunity from which, far more serious, disease?

A. Whooping cough
B. Polio
C. Smallpox
D. Chickenpox

5- John Harrison invented the marine chronometer. What did this invention enable sailors to accurately measure for the first time?

A: The speed of the ship
B: Latitude
C: Longitude
D: The depth of the water they are sailing in

Answer

**1- Sir Isaac Newton   2- Thomas Newcomen
3- The structure of atoms   4- Smallpox
5- Longitude**

1- What did British scientist Harry Brearley develop in 1913
that had first been suggested almost a century before?
A. Zinc-coated iron park railings
B. Mass-produced stainless steel
C. Aluminium cricket bats
D. Steel 'stay' wires for biplane aeroplane wings

2- In 1856 the British scientist Henry Bessemer made a breakthrough.
What did his 'Bessemer Process' achieve?
A. Turned lead into gold
B. Extracted hydrogen from air
C. Extracted petroleum spirit from crude oil
D. Turned pig iron into steel

3- "Raining, yes it's raining, These old blues are gaining ..." . Which Briton
invented the waterproof coat that bears his name 200 years later?
A. Charles Mackintosh
B. Gervais Puffer-Jacket
C. Henry Parka
D. John Duffel

4- Before 1837, means of quick communication were few. What was it that
harles Wheatstone and William Cook demonstrated that was to change all that?
A. Telephone exchanges
B. Hand-cranked signal mirror
C. Telegraph system
D. Semaphore flags

- The Aztecs were consuming chocolate products in South America. But it was not
ntil 1847 that a Briton created the first chocolate bar as we know it. Who was he?
A: Henri Nestlé
B: Joseph Fry
C: Milton S. Hershey
D: John Cadbury

Answer

1- "B"   2- Turned pig iron into steel
3- Charles Mackintosh   4- Telegraph system
5- Joseph Fry

1- What invention by the Briton Captain George William Manby in 1819 can be seen to this day in schools, factories, and offices?

A. *Portable fire extinguisher*
B. *Automated shoe polisher*
C. *Illuminated exit signs*
D. *Self-closing doors*

2- In 1934, a British inventor called Percy Shaw came up with an idea that was to become a life saver the world over. What did he invent?

A. *First wearable life jacket*
B. *Luminous paint*
C. *Cat's eyes on road*
D. *Plastic road bollard*

3- In 1967 the Briton John Shepard-Baron introduced the world to an innovation that was to revolutionise the world of finance. What was it?

A. *Visa card*
B. *The automated cheque stamp*
C. *Chequebook*
D. *Automated Teller Machine (ATM)*

4- In 1830, the Briton Edwin Budding invented a new tool that was to take the back-breaking effort out of a domestic chore. What was it?

A. *The Stinson wrench*
B. *The lawnmower*
C. *The pneumatic drill*
D. *The left-handed claw hammer*

5- In 1668, the reflecting telescope changed astronomy forever. It was the apple of one man's eye: who was that inventor?

A: *Richard Leigh*
B: *Christopher Brooke*
C: *Isaac Newton*
D: *Thomas Bancroft*

Answer

1- Portable fire extinguisher   2- Cat's eyes on road
3- ATM   4- The lawnmower
5- Isaac Newton

In days of yore, keeping food fresh was always a problem. What did Peter Durand invent in 1810 that paved the way for better longer term storage?

A. Tin can
B. Refrigeration
C. Salting process
D. Pickling process

2- In 1866, a Briton called Robert Whitehead invented a weapon that was to prove devastating in the cause of warfare. What was it?

A. Snipers' telescopic sight
B. Rifled artillery barrels
C. The bayonet
D. Self-propelled torpedo

3- In 1892 the British scientist James Dewar came up with an idea that became staple requirement for any outdoor picnic. What was it?

A. Plastic knives and forks
B. Unbreakable plates
C. Vacuum flask
D. Wicker hamper

4- In 1953, Christopher Cockerell came up with a new means of transport that was to find civilian and military uses. What was it?

A. Airwing
B. Hovercraft
C. Helicopter
D. Jet pack

5- Who was awarded the first patent for a pneumatic tyre?

A: Edward de Vere
B: Christopher Harvey
C: Robert William Thomson
D: John Boyd Dunlop

Answer

1- Tin can   2- Self-propelled torpedo
3- Vacuum flask   4- Hovercraft
5- Robert William Thomson

1- It was a light bulb moment: which Briton gave the world's first demonstration of a light bulb?
A. Joseph Swan
B. Goldsworthy Gurney
C. Louis Hartmann
D. Humphrey Davy

2- In 1820, the theory behind the electric motor was developed. However who was the Briton that, in 1821, turned theory into reality?
A. Frederick Walton
B. Michael Faraday
C. Charles Wheatstone
D. John Logie Baird

3- What was invented in 1733 that was to revolutionise weaving and kick start the Industrial Revolution?
A. Jacquard loom
B. Cotton gin
C. Water frame
D. Flying shuttle

4- Who invented the flying shuttle?
A. Richard Arkwright
B. Edmund Cartwright
C. John Kay
D. James Hargreaves

5- In 1824, a British mason called Joseph Aspdin came up with a variety that is noted today for its versatility and strength. What was it?
A: Portland cement
B: Stained glass
C: Wrought iron
D: Wooden trusses

Answer

1- Joseph Swan   2- Michael Faraday
3- Flying shuttle 4- John Kay
5- Portland cement

1- Who invented railway engine for the first time?
A. Robert Fulton
B. James Watt
C. George Stephenson
D. Richard Trevithick

2- In 1767, a British chemist called Joseph Priestly invented carbonated water. Where did he make his breakthrough?
A. In a monastery
B. In a winery
C. In a brewery
D. In a distillery

3- Which 1914 invention by the Briton Ernest Swinton was to change the way wars were fought for ever?
A. The hand grenade
B. The belt-fed machine gun
C. The flamethrower
D. The tank

4- In July 1996, a team of scientists and researchers made a breakthrough in genetics by cloning the first living animal. What was the clone's name?
A. Dolly
B. Golly
C. Molly
D. Polly

5- What home essential did the Briton Frederick Walton come up with in 1855 that has divided opinions ever since?
A: Water bed
B: Linoleum
C: Lego-proof slippers
D: Lazy Susan

Answer

1- George Stephenson   2- In a brewery
3- The tank   4- Dolly
5- Linoleum

1- What did John Walker develop in 1826 that improved efforts by others earlier?
A. Surgical scalpel
B. Left-handed screwdriver
C. Friction match
D. Stinson wrench

2- What was it that George Cayley invented in 1808 that improved the comfort for cyclists?
A. Tension spoked wheel
B. Five-speed gears
C. Sprung saddle
D. Gas-heated saddle

3- What did Sir Humphry Davy invent in 1807 that would ultimately be an enormous boon to the movie industry?
A. Auto-focus camera
B. Clapper board
C. Zoom lens
D. Arc lamp

4- What was the raw material used in the world's first factory, started by the Briton John Lombe in 1721?
A. Cotton
B. Silk
C. Wool
D. Linen

5- What did Richard Arkwright and John Kay develop in 1769 that has been described as "one of the greatest British inventions of all time"?
A: Heavier-than-air flight
B: Steel-tungsten scalpel
C: Spinning frame
D: Wireless radio transmission

Answer

1- Friction match   2- Tension spoked wheel
3- Arc lamp   4- Silk
5- Spinning frame

1- Who is the universally beloved naturalist and documentarian who has been working for the last seventy years?

A. *Alexander von Humboldt*
B. *Charles Darwin*
C. *David Attenborough*
D. *Steve Backshall*

2- What is the name of this inventor who created the first miners' safety lamp?

A. *Humphry Davy*
B. *Edith Humphrey*
C. *Anna Atkins*
D. *Bertha Swirles*

3- Who is the inventor of the Victorian period who pioneered the first "computer"?

A. *Maurice Wilkes*
B. *Charles Babbage*
C. *Grace Hopper*
D. *Alan Turing*

4- When you feel minty fresh, who do you thank for inventing the mass-produced toothbrush?

A. *William Addis*
B. *James Goodfellow*
C. *Joseph Friedman*
D. *Melitta Bentz*

5- Can you name the industrial-era entrepreneur who figured out how to make a cotton-carding machine?

A: *Richard Arkwright*
B: *James Hargreaves*
C: *Eli Whitney*
D: *Samuel Morse*

Answer

1- David Attenborough   2- Humphry Davy
3- Charles Babbage   4- William Addis
5- Richard Arkwright

1- Do you know this inventor who created the seed drill?
A. Jethro Tull
B. John Deere
C. Edmund Quincy
D. Joseph Dart

2- Who is this towering figure in the Industrial Revolution, builder of the Rocket locomotive?
A. Thomas Boulsover
B. William Symington
C. Christiaan Huygens
D. George Stephenson

3- What was Alexander Graham Bell's first invention?
A. Camera
B. Lamp
C. Telephone
D. Telegraph

4- This Scottish-born industrialist was a key figure in building American railroads and factories. Who is he?
A. Charles Crocker
B. Daniel Drew
C. John Jacob Astor
D. Andrew Carnegie

5- This famous physicist is noted for his book "A Brief History of Time." What is his name?
A: Stephen Hawking
B: Albert Einstein
C: Max Planck
D: Ernest Rutherford

Answer
1- Jethro Tull 2- George Stephenson
3- Telephone 4- Andrew Carnegie
5- Stephen Hawking

1- In computer networking, what does the IP stand for in the acronym TCP/IP?

A. Inferior packet

B. Instruction pointer

C. iPod

D. Internet protocol

2- Bubonic plague is one of three types of plague and is mainly spread how?

A. Fleas from animals

B. Coughing and sneezing

C. Undercooked meat

D. Contaminated water

3- What type of computer virus takes its name from mythology?

A. Achilles heel

B. Odyssey

C. Trojan horse

D. Apple of Discord

4- What number system does a microprocessor use?

A. Octal

B. Binary

C. Hexadecimal

D. Decimal

5- Codenamed "Longhorn", which operating system did Microsoft release initially in 2006 and generally in 2007?

A: Windows 7

B: Windows Vienna

C: Windows XP

D: Windows Vista

Answer

1- Internet protocol   2- Fleas from animals
3- Trojan horse   4- Binary
5- Windows Vista

Art
&
Literature

1- What Elizabethan author of "The Passionate Shepherd to His Love"
died in a barroom brawl?
A. John Lyly
B. Christopher Marlowe
C. Thomas Champion
D. Ben Johnson

2- What adventure-loving writer/poet was beheaded?
A. Sir Walter Raleigh
B. Henry Woodsman
C. Count Don Juan
D. Prince Henry

3- Who or what was the subject of Edmund Spenser's
"The Faerie Queene"?
A. Camelot
B. A supernatural ruler
C. Elizabeth I
D. James II

4- What was an occupation of John Donne,
the author of "Death, Be Not Proud"?
A. Coachman
B. Roman Catholic bishop
C. Anglican preacher
D. Saloon keeper

5- Which author, philosopher and essayist rose to the position
of Lord Chancellor under King James I?
A: Eli Pepper
B: Francis Bacon
C: Barth Toast
D: Roger Hamm

Answer

1- Christopher Marlowe   2- Sir Walter Raleigh
3- Elizabeth I   4- Anglican preacher
5- Francis Bacon

1- Best known for his depiction of industrial areas, L. S. Lowry set the majority of his paintings in which area of the United Kingdom?
A. Welsh Valleys
B. London
C. Northwest England
D. Scottish Highlands

2- Painting portraits, often an artist will request that the models remain in positio for extended periods. Which of these artists is best remembered for his portraits?
A. David Hockney
B. Samuel Palmer
C. Lucian Freud
D. John Constable

3- One of the foremost figures in 20th Century British art, Barbara Hepworth led a colony of artists in which Cornish town from World War II onwards?
A. St. Ives
B. Falmouth
C. Newquay
D. Bude

4- Augustus John, known for his etchings and portraits, was born in which country of the UK?
A. England
B. Wales
C. Scotland
D. Northern Ireland

5- 'Peace - Burial at Sea' and 'The Fighting Temeraire'
They are works by which artist?
A: Ford Madox Brown
B: J. M. W. Turner
C: Samuel Palmer
D: William Etty

Answer

1- Northwest England   2- Lucian Freud
3- St. Ives 4- Wales
5- J. M. W. Turner

1- Which of the following was not one of the Cavalier Poets?
A. John Suckling
B. Robert Herrick
C. Richard Lovelace
D. William Blake

2- Poet John Milton composed "Paradise Lost" while under what physical handicap?
A. Deafness
B. Epilepsy
C. Insanity
D. Blindness

3- In what work by John Bunyan does one find Vanity Fair and Sloughs of Despond?
A. Elizabeth the Queen
B. Beowulf
C. The Pilgrim's Progress
D. The Canterbury Tales

4- The diary of which Secretary of the Admiralty gives first-hand accounts of the plague of 1665 and the Great Fire of London?
A. Edward Jonson
B. Paul Daniel Samuels
C. Daniel Beckett
D. Samuel Pepys

5- Who is considered by many as the chief poet and playwright of the Restoration as well as the father of modern English prose?
A: Edwin Rorden
B: John Dryden
C: Philip Matthews
D: Robert Heiden

Answer
1- William Blake   2- Blindness
3- The Pilgrim's Progress   4- Samuel Pepys
5- John Dryden

1- Which member of the Young British Artists submitted a piece entitled 'My Bed' when she was nominated for the Turner Prize in 1999?

A. Tracey Emin

B. Sarah Lucas

C. Fiona Rae

D. Georgina Starr

2- William Holman Hunt was one the founders of which British art movement?

A. Stuckism

B. Manchester School of Painters

C. Pre-Raphaelite Brotherhood

D. Vorticism

3- Which of these British sculptors is easily recognised by his large, somewhat abstract, reclining figures cast in bronze?

A. Anthony Caro

B. Henry Moore

C. Eric Gill

D. Anish Kapoor

4- Which artist, born in Liverpool, is best known for his depictions of horses

A. George Stubbs

B. George Gower

C. Samuel Cooper

D. Peter Lely

5- Which of these artists was also a great poet, and produced illustration to accompany his 'Songs of Innocence'?

A: William Blake

B: Samuel Palmer

C: John Crome

D: Joseph Wright of Derby

* *

Answer

1- Tracey Emin   2- Pre-Raphaelite Brotherhood
3- Henry Moore   4- George Stubbs
5- William Blake

* *

1- Who or what was Beowulf?
A. A King of the Danes
B. An Anglo-Saxon soldier
C. A Geatish warrior
D. A half-man half-wolf monster

2- Who did Beowulf slay?
A. Grendel
B. Hrothgar
C. Hygelac
D. Geats

3- Over who or what was Beowulf's final victory?
A. Wiglaf
B. Grendel's son
C. Saxon invaders
D. A dragon

4- In "The Canterbury Tales" where did the pilgrims meet up before their journey?
A. Tower of London
B. London Bridge
C. Inns of Court
D. Tabard Inn

5- Where in Canterbury was the final destination for the pilgrims in "The Canterbury Tales"?
A: The shrine of Thomas Becket
B: The palace of King Edward III
C: Westminster Abbey
D: The palace of the Archbishop of Canterbury

Answer
1- a Geatish warrior   2- Grendel
3- A dragon   4- Tabard Inn
5- The shrine of Thomas Becket

1- "The Blue Boy" (1779).
A. Thomas Gainsborough
B. Joshua Reynolds
C. Thomas Lawrence
D. John Constable

2- "The Gate of Calais" (1748).
A. William Blake
B. William Hogarth
C. J. M. W. Turner
D. Thomas Gainsborough

3- "Girl with a Kitten" (1947).
A. Caspar David Friedrich
B. John Constable
C. Francis Bacon
D. Lucian Freud

4- "The Physical Impossibility of Death in the Mind of Someone Living" (1991
A. Jeff Koons
B. Damien Hirst
C. Andy Warhol
D. David Hockney

5- "House" (1993).
A: Rachel Whiteread
B: Marcus Taylor
C: Sarah Lucas
D: Eva Hesse

Answer

1- Thomas Gainsborough   2- William Hogarth
3- Lucian Freud   4- Damien Hirst
5- Rachel Whiteread

1 - Who teamed with Joseph Addison to form the famous literary partnership that put out the news sheet "The Tatler" and the daily paper "The Spectator"?
A. Samuel Richards
B. John Barrington
C. Albert Samuels
D. Richard Steele

2 - Prior to writing "Robinson Crusoe" what was Daniel Defoe's profession?
A. Priest
B. Government worker
C. Journalist
D. Sea captain

3 - Where was Jonathan Swift, the author of "Gulliver's Travels", born?
A. Malta
B. Ireland
C. England
D. Wales

4 - From what physical deformity did the great poet Alexander Pope suffer?
A. Hunchback
B. One arm
C. One leg
D. Shrivelled arm

5 - If you wanted to learn about well-bred manners and fashion, which Eighteenth Century critic's work would you read?
A: Lord Kent
B: Lord Winston
C: Lord Marlboro
D: Lord Chesterfield

Answer

1- Richard Steele   2- Journalist
3- Ireland   4- Hunchback
5- Lord Chesterfield

1- "Three Studies for Figures at the Base of a Crucifixion" (1944).
A. *Stanley Spencer*
B. *David Hockney*
C. *William Blake*
D. *Francis Bacon*

2- "Beatrice Addressing Dante from the Car" (1824-7).
A. *Johan Zoffany*
B. *William Blake*
C. *Peter Blake*
D. *John Constable*

3- "The Derby Day" (1856-58).
A. *William Holman Hunt*
B. *John Singer Sargent*
C. *Sir Lawrance Alma-Tadema*
D. *William Powell Frith*

4- "A Bigger Splash" (1967).
A. *David Hockney*
B. *Henry Moore*
C. *Dame Barbara Hepworth*
D. *Damien Hurst*

5- "Merry-Go-Round" (1916).
A: *Henry Moore*
B: *Eric Gill*
C: *Paul Nash*
D: *Mark Gertler*

1- What did Samuel Johnson publish in 1755 that established his reputation as a scholar and writer?

A. Book of Poems
B. Critical essays
C. Planetary study
D. Dictionary

2- Which of the following was not written by Oliver Goldsmith?

A. She Stoops to Conquer
B. The Deserted Village
C. The Vicar of Wakefield
D. Elizabeth the Queen

3- Where did Thomas Grey write his famous "Elegy"?

A. A prison
B. A boarding house
C. A seashore
D. A country churchyard

4- What was Robert Burns' "luve" like?

A. A dying ember
B. A red, red rose
C. A full, full moon
D. A springtime morn

5- In one of William Blake's most famous poems he wrote about what animal "burning bright"?

A: Lion
B: Dove
C: Tiger
D: Sparrow

Answer

1- Dictionary   2- Elizabeth the Queen
3- A country churchyard   4- A red, red rose
5- Tiger

1- "Self-Portrait with Badges" (1961).
A. John Piper
B. William Blake
C. Paul Nash
D. Peter Blake

2- "Ophelia" (1851-52).
A. Dante Gabriel Rossett
B. Sir John Everett Millais, Bt
C. George Frederic Watts
D. Joseph Mallord William Turner

3- "Girl with a Parrot" (1670).
A. William Hogarth
B. Sir Peter Lely
C. Sir Anthony van Dyke
D. Sir Godfrey Kneller

4- "Mares and Foals in a River Landscape" (1763-68).
A. John William Waterhouse
B. Sir Edwin Landseer
C. George Stubbs
D. Henry Fuseli

5- "Peace - Burial at Sea" (1842).
A: Ford Madox Brown
B: Joseph Mallord William Turner
C: Thomas Gainsborough
D: Sir David Wilkie

Answer

1- Peter Blake   2- Sir John Everett Millais, Bt
3- Sir Peter Lely 4- George Stubbs
5- Joseph Mallord William Turner

1- Which George Eliot novel is subtitled 'A Study Of Provincial Life'?
   A. Silas Marner
   B. Adam Bede
   C. Middlemarch
   D. The Mill On The Floss

- Which Austen novel was originally called "First Impressions"?
   A. Emma
   B. Mansfield Park
   C. Sense and Sensibility
   D. Pride and Prejudice

3- Whom does Emma take under her wing in the novel
   of the same name?
   A. Heidi Smith
   B. Harriet Smith
   C. Harvey Smith
   D. Henryetta Smith

4- Which Austen novel was first called "Elinor and Marianne"?
   A. Emma
   B. Northanger Abbey
   C. Sense and Sensibility
   D. Persuasion

5- Who played Elizabeth Bennet in British TV's
   "Pride and Prejudice" in 1995?
   A. Jennifer Ehle
   B. Jodie Ehle
   C. Jennifer Earle
   D. Jodie Earle

Answer

1- Middlemarch   2- Pride and Prejudice
3- Harriet Smith   4- Sense and Sensibility
5- Jennifer Ehle

British Music

1- "Young Parisians", "Car Trouble" and "Deutscher Girls".
Which band had hits with these songs?
A. The Clash
B. Adam and the Ants
C. The Buzzcocks
D. XTC

2- Can you name the lead singer of 80s band "Altered Images"?
A. Debbie Harry
B. Clare Grogan
C. Patsy Kensit
D. None of these

3- Which band had hits with "Oblivious", "Somewhere in my Heart"
and "Good Morning Britain"?
A. The Apartments
B. The Associates
C. Aztec Camera
D. Orange Juice

4- Can you remember the tune that "Babybird" had a huge hit with?
A. You're Gorgeous
B. Goodnight
C. Bad Old Man
D. Candygirl

5- "Song for Whoever", "We are each other" and "Don't Marry Her"
came from which band?
A: The Housemartins
B: Duran Duran
C: The Beautiful South
D: The Beat

Answer
1- Adam and the Ants   2- Clare Grogan
3- Aztec Camera   4- You're Gorgeous
5- The Beautiful South

1- On which "Belle and Sebastian" album would you find the songs "I'm a Cuckoo" and "Step into my Office Baby"?

A. Tigermilk
B. The Boy With The Arab Strap
C. Storytelling
D. Dear Catastrophe Waitress

2- Which 70s punk band had hits with "What do I Get" and "Orgasm Addict"?

A. The Damned
B. The Buzzcocks
C. The Sex Pistols
D. The Clash

3- Which band's songs are these: "C'30, C'60, C'90, Go", "Your Cassette Pet" and "Chihuahua"?

A. The Cure
B. Culture Club
C. Bow Wow Wow
D. Adam and the Ants

4- "Bank Robber", "I Fought the Law" and "White Riot": Which band had hits with these songs?

A. The Vapours
B. The Clash
C. The Jam
D. The Sex Pistols

5- Which singer had hits with "Sexuality", "Levi Stubb's Tears" and "She's Leaving Home"?

A. Billy Bragg
B. Morrissey
C. David Gray
D. Billy Childish

Answer

1- Dear Catastrophe Waitress   2- The Buzzcocks
3- Bow Wow Wow   4- The Clash
5- Billy Bragg

1- Which UK singer did The Cardigans collaborate with
on their hit single 'Burning Down the House'?
A. Julian Cope
B. David Gray
C. Tom Jones
D. None of these

2- 'What a Waste', 'I Want to be Straight'
and 'Hit me with your Rhythm Stick'. Which Band?
A. Fun Boy Three
B. Ian Dury and the Blockheads
C. Madness
D. The Specials

3- Which Liverpudlian band had hits in the 80s with 'Rescue',
'The Cutter' and 'A Promise'?
A. The Zutons
B. Echo and the Bunnymen
C. Cast
D. Teardrop Explodes

4- On which 'Goldfrapp' album would you find these songs
'Deep Honey', 'Strict Machine' and 'Train'?
A. Black Cherry
B. Felt Mountain
C. Supernature
D. None of these

5- Which band sang these songs: 'Get Myself Arrested'
and 'Rhythm and Blues Alibi'?
A. The Zutons
B. Babyshambles
C. The Libertines
D. Gomez

Answer
1- Tom Jones   2- "B"
3- Echo and the Bunnymen   4- Black Cherry
5- Gomez

1- Which Bob Dylan song did P J Harvey cover on her 'Rid Of Me' album?
A. Highway 61 Revisited
B. Desolation Row
C. It Ain't me Babe
D. Shot of Love

2- 'I Don't Know Why I Love You' and 'Shine On' were hits for which band
A. Happy Mondays
B. The Inspiral Carpets
C. The Stone Roses
D. House Of Love

3- Which was the only Housemartins single to top the UK charts?
A. Think for a Minute
B. Caravan of Love
C. Happy Hour
D. Me and the Farmer

**4- Remember Madchester? Which band had hits
with 'This is how it Feels', 'Joe' and 'Please be Cruel'?**
A. Inspiral Carpets
B. The Happy Mondays
C. Pop Will Eat Itself
D. House of Love

**5- 'News of the World', 'The Eton Rifles'
and 'That's Entertainment', were hits for which UK band?**
A. XTC
B. The Jam
C. The Police
D. The Stranglers

Answer

1- Highway 61 Revisited   2- House Of Love
3- Caravan of Love   4- Inspiral Carpets
5- The Jam

- 'In the Year 2525' was a huge hit in the UK and in America for whom?
  A. Fifth Dimension
  B. Edwin Starr
  C. Zager and Evans
  D. The Foundations

2- 'Je T'aime Moi Non Plus' was a raunchy hit for whom?
  A. Jane Birkin and Serge Gainsbourg
  B. Henry Mancini and his Orchestra
  C. New Colony Six
  D. Cuff Links

3- 'Spirit in the Sky' has been covered by numerous artists over the years, who was the original one hit wonder?
  A. Bobby Sherman
  B. Norman Greenbaum
  C. Ray Stevens
  D. B.J Thomas

4- 'Wandrin' Star' was a number one hit for which Academy Award winning actor?
  A. Ron Moody
  B. Alan Arkin
  C. Rod Steiger
  D. Lee Marvin

5- Which British actor had a hit with 'Grandad' in 1971?
  A. John Laurie
  B. Arthur Lowe
  C. Clive Dunn
  D. Ian Lavender

Answer

1- Zager and Evans   2- "A"
3- Norman Greenbaum   4- Lee Marvin
5- Clive Dunn

1- 'Float On' was a UK one hit wonder for which American band?

A. Marshall Tucker Band

B. Sylvers

C. The Floaters

D. Emotions

2- 'Uptown Top Ranking' was a surprise hit in 1978 for who?

A. Althea and Donna

B. The Abyssinians

C. Rita Marley

D. Smiley Culture

3- 'Matchstalk Men and Matchstalk Cats and Dogs' was a tribute to the artist L.S Lowry, it was a hit in 1978 for whom?

A. Jan and Dean

B. Sam and Dave

C. Flo and Eddie

D. Brian and Michael

4- 'Pump up the Volume' was a big hit in 1987 for which house music ac

A. Steve 'Silk' Hurley

B. S'Express

C. M/A/R/R/S

D. Yazz and the Plastic Population

5- If you've got children, chances are they loved this tune: 'Do you Really Like it', it was a hit in 2001 for who?

A. DJ Casper

B. DJ Pied Piper and the Master of Ceremonies

C. DJ Otzi

D. DJ Sammy & Yanou featuring Do

Answer

1- The Floaters   2- Althea and Donna

3- Brian and Michael 4- M/A/R/R/S

5- DJ Pied Piper and the Master of Ceremonies

1- "Stand and Deliver" (1981).
A. Culture Club
B. Diana Dors
C. Adam and the Ants
D. Bow Wow Wow

2- "Someone Like You" (2011).
A. Ed Sheeran
B. Adele
C. Sam Smith
D. Bruno Mars

3- "(If Paradise Is) Half as Nice" (1969).
A. Jamiroquai
B. Fair Weather
C. Strawbs
D. Amen Corner

4- "I Bet You Look Good on the Dancefloor" (2005).
A. Arctic Monkeys
B. The Neighbourhood
C. The Strokes
D. Gorillaz

5- "Hallelujah" (2008).
A. Alexandra Burke
B. Melissa Bell
C. Leona Lewis
D. Diana Vickers

Answer

1- Adam and the Ants   2- Adele
3- Amen Corner 4- Arctic Monkeys
5- Alexandra Burke

Who Am I?

1- I had a UK number one hit single with "Evergreen".

A. Gareth Gates
B. Will Young
C. Eg White
D. Camille O'Sullivan

2- I was the youngest member of One Direction.

A. Niall Horan
B. Zayn Malik
C. Harry Styles
D. Louis Tomlinson

3- My first single was called "Those Were the Days".

A. Mary Hopkin
B. Jessica Lee Morgan
C. Clodagh Rodgers
D. Sandie Shaw

4- I was part of a group who won Popstars: The Rivals.

A. Jade Thirlwall
B. Kimberley Walsh
C. Perrie Edwards
D. Leigh-Anne Pinnock

5- I was the first winner of "Britain's Got Talent".

A. Lee Ridley
B. Jai McDowall
C. George Sampson
D. Paul Potts

Answer

1- Will Young   2- Harry Styles
3- Mary Hopkin 4- Kimberley Walsh
5- Paul Potts

Who Am I?

1- My first album was called "Spirit".
A. Calum Scott
B. Leona Lewis
C. Alexandra Burke
D. Natasha Bedingfield

2- I was born Marie McDonald McLaughlin Lawrie.
A. Lulu
B. Maurice Gibb
C. John Frieda
D. Jordan Frieda

3- I often sat "Under the Moon of Love" wearing my Teddy Boy outfit.
A. Bay City Rollers
B. Mud
C. The Rubettes
D. Showaddywaddy

4- I walked on sunshine and it felt really good.
"Album: Walking on Sunshine / 1983"
A. Pablo Cruise
B. Katrina And The Waves
C. Bucks Fizz
D. Ying Yang Twins

5- I won the 1976 Eurovision Song Contest.
A. Edison Lighthouse
B. Bucks Fizz
C. Brotherhood of Man
D. White Plains

Answer

1- Leona Lewis   2- Lulu
3- Showaddywaddy 4- Katrina And The Waves
5- Brotherhood of Man

1- What fast instrumental was a UK number one hit for B. Bumble and The Stingers in May 1962?

A. Bumble Boogie
B. Apache
C. Nut Rocker
D. Telstar

2- "Michelle" was a UK one hit wonder for The Overlanders in 1966. Who recorded the original version of the song?

A. The Rolling Stones
B. The Hollies
C. The Beatles
D. The Kinks

3- Which 1968 single was a one hit wonder for The Crazy World of Arthur Brown?

A. Air
B. Fire
C. Water
D. Earth

4- In 1977 The Floaters had a UK one hit wonder with what single?

A. Float On
B. In The Stars
C. Astrology
D. Let's Float

5- Which American singer had a hit in 1982 with the song "I've Never Been To Me"?

A. Brandy
B. Nicole
C. Charlene
D. Lulu

Answer

1- Nut Rocker   2- The Beatles
3- Fire   4- Float On
5- Charlene

1- Which duo scored a hit with 'Barbados' in 1975?

A. Typically Tropical
B. The Tymes
C. Doobie Brothers
D. Average White Band

Which one hit wonder released the disco classic, 'Ring my Bell', in 1979?

A. Donna Summer
B. Maureen McGovern
C. Anita Ward
D. Mary MacGregor

- 'The Stonk', was a number one hit in 1991 for which comedy duo?

A. Cannon and Ball
B. Little and Large
C. Reeves and Mortimer
D. Hale and Pace

4- 'Baby Cakes' was a huge hit in 2004 for which dance act?

A. DJ Casper
B. 3 of a Kind
C. Eric Prydz
D. Usher

5- 'Cool for Cats', 'Up the Junction' and 'Labelled With Love' were hits for which band?

A. Squeeze
B. The Stranglers
C. 10cc
D. XTC

Answer

1- Typically Tropical   2- Anita Ward
3- Hale and Pace   4- 3 of a Kind
5- Squeeze

Sport

Football:

1- Who won the 2016 Premier League title?
A. Manchester City
B. Chelsea
C. Liverpool
D. Manchester United

2- Which of the following is not a football ground?
A. Etihad Stadium
B. Villa Park
C. Goodison Park
D. Brighton

3- What team was Charlie George a legendary player for?
A. Manchester United
B. Tottenham Hotspur
C. Arsenal
D. West Ham United

4- Who has won most caps for England?
A. Steven Gerrard
B. Peter Shilton
C. Wayne Rooney
D. David Beckham

5- What was the first English club to win the European Cup?
A. Liverpool
B. Manchester United
C. Nottingham Forest
D. Aston Villa

Answer
1- Chelsea   2- Brighton
3- Arsenal 4- Peter Shilton "(125 Caps)
5- Manchester United (1967–68)

Premier League:

1- Who won the 2020-21 Premier League title?
A. Liverpool
B. Manchester United
C. Manchester City
D. Chelsea

2- Which club finished top of the Premiership in the 2019-20 season
A. Liverpool
B. Manchester United
C. Liverpool
D. Chelsea

3- Who was the top scorer in the 2019-20 EPL season?
A. Raheem Sterling
B. Harry Kane
C. Jamie Vardy
D. Sadio Mané

4- Who won the Premier League in 2015–16?
A. Manchester United
B. Chelsea
C. Leicester City
D. Manchester City

5- Which player won the Golden Boot in the 2020-21?
A. Jamie Vardy
B. Jack Grealish
C. Mohamed Salah
D. Harry Kane

Answer

1- Manchester City   2- Liverpool
3- Jamie Vardy
4- Leicester City   5- Harry Kane

Football Stadiums:

1- What is the home ground of Chelsea?
A. Fulham Road
B. Ibrox
C. Stamford Bridge
D. Portman Road

2- What is the home ground of Manchester United?
A. Lazer Stadium
B. The Oval
C. The Theatre of Dreams
D. Old Trafford

3- What was the home ground of Arsenal, before they moved to a new home ground in 2006?
A. Hyde Field
B. Highbury
C. Emirates Stadium
D. Plumstead Common

4- Where do Liverpool play their home games?
A. Merseyside
B. Goodison Park
C. Stanley Park
D. Anfield

5- Where did Tottenham Hotspur play their home games for 118 years?
A. White Hart Lane
B. Northumberland Park
C. Paxton Road
D. Hotspur Stadium

Answer

1- Stamford Bridge   2- Old Trafford
3- Highbury   4- Anfield
5- White Hart Lane

Rugby League Nicknames:

1- The Wire.
A. St. Helens
B. Wakefield Trinity
C. Warrington Wolves
D. Wigan Warriors

2- The Loiners.
A. Leigh Centurions
B. Newcastle Thunder
C. Leeds Rhinos
D. Salford Red Devils

3- The Glassblowers.
A. Salford Red Devils
B. Catalan Dragons
C. Hull Kingston Rovers
D. Castleford Tigers

4- The Chemics.
A. Whitehaven
B. Widnes Vikings
C. York City Knights
D. Toulouse Olympique

5- The Gallant Youths.
A. Featherstone Rovers
B. Dewsbury Rams
C. Batley Bulldogs
D. Barrow Raiders

Answer
1- Warrington Wolves   2- Leeds Rhinos
3- Castleford Tigers   4- Widnes Vikings
5- Batley Bulldogs

Rugby League Nicknames:

1- The Shipbuilders.
A. Barrow Raiders
B. Batley Bulldogs
C. Dewsbury Rams
D. Halifax

2- The Fartowners.
A. Hull Kingston Rovers
B. Huddersfield Giants
C. Hull F.C.
D. Leigh Centurions

3- The Riversiders.
A. St. Helens
B. Wakefield Trinity
C. Wigan Warriors
D. Warrington Wolves

4- The Lawkholmers.
A. Keighley Cougars
B. Hunslet
C. Doncaster
D. Coventry Bears

5- Northern.
A. Bradford Bulls
B. Barrow Raiders
C. Batley Bulldogs
D. Dewsbury Rams

Answer

1- Barrow Raiders   2- Huddersfield Giants
3- Wigan Warriors   4- Keighley Cougars
5- Bradford Bulls

Wimbledon:

1- In 2010, which player upset both Roger Federer and Novak Djokovic on his way to a final loss to Rafael Nadal?

A. Tomas Berdych

B. David Ferrer

C. Robin Soderling

D. Stan Wawrinka

2- In 2014, Novak Djokovic won a thrilling five-set final against which player?

A. Roger Federer

B. Rafael Nadal

C. Andy Murray

3- Roger Federer won his eighth Wimbledon title in 2017 with victory over which player in the final?

A. Jo-Wilfried Tsonga

B. Lucas Pouille

C. Marin Cilic

D. Alexander Zverev

4- In 2018, which player won her first women's singles title with victory over Serena Williams in the final?

A. Sloane Stephens

B. Naomi Osaka

C. Angelique Kerber

D. Jelena Ostapenko

5- Serena Williams lost the women's final in 2018 and lost again in the 2019 final. Who beat her in 2019, for her first Wimbledon crown

A. Simona Halep

B. Ashleigh Barty

C. Karolina Pliskova

Answer

1- Tomas Berdych   2- Roger Federer
3- Marin Cilic   4- Angelique Kerber
5- Simona Halep

Queens of the Centre Court & Their nationality:

1- Maud Watson.
A. American
B. British
C. French
D. Australian

2- May Sutton.
A. Czech
B. Swiss
C. American
D. French

3- Maria Sharapova.
A. Bosnia and Herzegovina
B. Australian
C. Czech
D. Russian

4- Jana Novotna.
A. German
B. Brazilian
C. Czech
D. Spanish

5- Martina Hingis.
A. French
B. Swiss
C. American
D. British

Answer

1- British 2- American
3- Russian 4- Czech
5- Swiss

Golf:

1-Which three British golfers all hit the world no. 1 spot in 2011 or 2012?

A. Colin Montgomerie, Rory McIlroy and Ian Poulter
B. Luke Donald, Luke Donald and Lee Westwood
C. Luke Donald, Rory McIlroy and Lee Westwood
D. Lee Westwood, Rory McIlroy and Tony Jacklin

2- Who, in 2011, became the all-time leading points scorer in the Solheim Cup?

A. Juli Inkster
B. Laura Davies
C. Karrie Webb
D. Annika Sörenstam

3- Who, in 1969, was the first British winner of the Open Championship for eighteen years?

A. Jack Nicklaus
B. Tony Jacklin
C. Sam Torrance
D. Lee Trevino

4- Who was the youngest when they won their first Major?

A. Rory McIlroy
B. Tiger Woods
C. Steve Stricker

5- What is the common name given to the championship golf course known formally as the Royal Liverpool Golf Club?

A. Hoylake
B. West Kirby
C. Heswall
D. Wallasey

Answer

1- "C"   2- Laura Davies
3- Tony Jacklin   4- Tiger Woods
5- Hoylake

Boxing:

1- Which British boxer came to public attention when he won the silver medal in the lightweight division at the 2004 Olympics?
   A. Younus Khan
   B. Amir Khan
   C. Imran Khan
   D. Zaheer Khan

2- Barry McGuigan was known by which nickname during his boxing career?
   A. The Celtic Warrior
   B. The Jackal
   C. The Hitman
   D. The Clones Cyclone

3- Which former British boxing champion was known for his lisp and eccentric dress sense?
   A. Alan Minter
   B. Lloyd Honeyghan
   C. David Haye
   D. Chris Eubank

4- Which former English cricketer made his boxing debut in 2012 in the heavyweight division?
   A. Graham Gooch
   B. Ian Botham
   C. Andrew Flintoff
   D. Michael Vaughan

5- The 2012 Olympics saw women's boxing included for the first time. Who won the gold medal for Britain?
   A. Laura Trott
   B. Nicola Adams
   C. Jessica Ennis
   D. Katherine Grainger

Answer

1- Amir Khan   2- The Clones Cyclone
3- Chris Eubank   4- Andrew Flintoff
5- Nicola Adams

Boxing:

1- Former lightweight boxing champion Ken Buchanan was born in which country of the UK?
A. Wales
B. Scotland
C. Northern Ireland
D. England

2- Which British heavyweight boxing champion was almost as well known for his expression 'now what I mean 'arry?' as for his boxing ability?
A. Jack Bodell
B. Brian London
C. Frank Bruno
D. Joe Bugner

3- British heavyweight boxing champion Henry Cooper famously floored which fighter in a 1963 bout?
A. Sonny Liston
B. Ingemar Johansson
C. Floyd Patterson
D. Muhammad Ali

4- 'The Dark Destroyer' was the nickname of which former British world boxing champion?
A. Chris Pyatt
B. Carl Froch
C. Nigel Benn
D. Joe Calzaghe

5- Who did Randy Turpin defeat to become British Middleweight champion in 1950?
A. Albert Finch
B. Gilbert Stock
C. Pete Mead
D. William Poli

Answer
**1- Scotland   2- Frank Bruno
3- Muhammad Ali   4- Nigel Benn
5- Albert Finch**

The UK Football Players:

What is the name of the English club David Beckham first joined in 1992?

A. AC Milan
B. Real Madrid
C. Manchester United
D. Tottenham Hotspur

2- Who did Steve McManaman play international football for?

A. England
B. Northern Ireland
C. Scotland
D. Wales

3- Which country is Colin Hendry from?

A. Wales
B. Scotland
C. Northern Ireland
D. England

4- Nathan Blake was capped by which country?

A. Wales
B. Ireland
C. Scotland
D. Northern Ireland

- Keith Gillespie was an international star for which national team?

A. Wales
B. Scotland
C. Ireland
D. Northern Ireland

Answer

1- Manchester United   2- England
3- Scotland 4- Wales
5- Northern Ireland

Entertainment

1- Who was the first Dr Who?

A. Patrick Troughton
B. William Hartnell
C. Jon Pertwee
D. Peter Cushing

2- Who was the original Master on the TV show?

A. Roger Rees
B. Roger DeCorsey
C. Roger Delgado
D. Roger Whittaker

3- In Space 1999, who played John Koenig?

A. Nick Tate
B. Barry Morse
C. Tony Anholt
D. Martin Landau

4- What organization did Captain Scarlet work for?

A. RAINBOW
B. SHADO
C. SPECTRUM
D. MYSTERONS

5- Who is the alien with two heads in 'A Hitch Hikers Guide To The Galaxy'?

A. Ford Prefect
B. Trillian
C. Slartibartfast
D. Zaphod Beeblebrox

Answer

1- William Hartnell   2- Roger Delgado
3- Martin Landau   4- SPECTRUM
5- Zaphod Beeblebrox

Follow the clues & Identify the show:

1- Like watching paint dry / Waiting for coins to drop off Infernal machine!

A. Pressure Point
B. Tipping Point
C. Drop Zone
D. The Edge

2- Fifteen contestants / Get too many questions wrong And your lights are out!

A. Last Man Standing
B. Every Second Counts
C. Wipeout
D. Fifteen To One

3- Hosted by Holness / 'Can I have a 'P' please Bob?' / It's two against one.

A. Blockbusters
B. Double Cross
C. Chain Letters
D. Catchphrase

4- Eight frightened students / Faced With Jeremy Paxman. Your starter for ten.

A. University Challenge
B. Student Showdown
C. The Third Degree
D. College Bowl

5- Sat in big black chair / Being Quizzed by John Humphrys. Approaching menace.

A. Ejector Seat
B. Mastermind
C. Pressure Point
D. The Chair

Answer

**1- Tipping Point   2- Fifteen To One
3- Blockbusters   4- University Challenge
5- Mastermind**

Follow the clues & Identify the show:

1- Go fifty/fifty? I could ask the audience / I could phone a friend.
A. *Who Wants To Be A Millionaire?*
B. *The Link*
C. *Perfection*
D. *Ask The Family*

2- Lowest scorers win / Wrong answers score a hundred. No points are required.
A. *Family Fortunes*
B. *The Edge*
C. *Pointless*
D. *No Win No Fee*

3- Five plucky players / Take on the quiz goliaths Scrambled, boiled or fried?
A. *Brain Drain*
B. *Eggheads*
C. *Think Tank*
D. *Brain of Britain*

4- Obscure connections / Behind Egyptian letters Vowels are missing?
A. *The Wall*
B. *The Link*
C. *Twister*
D. *Only Connect*

5- Will it be 'The Beast? Or perhaps 'The Governess'? It's 'The Sinnerman'!?
A. *Golden Balls*
B. *The Chase*
C. *The Fuse*
D. *Ejector Seat*

Answer

**1- Who Wants To Be A Millionaire?. 2- Pointless
3- Eggheads 4- Only Connect
5- The Chase**

1- I played the role of Dr. Watson in the 2009 film 'Sherlock Holmes'.
I have also produced and acted in a 2007 film starring Michael Caine?
A. Hugh Laurie
B. Jude Law
C. Hugh Grant
D. Colin Firth

2- I was cast for my first movie at the age of nine.
I played the role of a 'muggle-born' young witch?
A. Maggie Smith
B. Daniel Radcliffe
C. Emma Watson
D. Rupert Grint

3- I made my debut in the 1985 film 'The Good Father'. In the 2010 film
'Alice in Wonderland', I voiced the character of Cheshire Cat?
A. Johnny Depp
B. Hugh Laurie
C. Colin Firth
D. Stephen Fry

4- This first detective is known by only one name which describes
a code for sending messages. Who was he?
A. Morse
B. Hope
C. Pasco
D. Hathaway

5- Which of the choices was a Scotland Yard police officer
who sometimes appeared in the Sherlock Holmes stories
A. Inspector Barlow
B. Inspector Lestrade
C. Inspector Lindley
D. Inspector Japp

Answer

1- Jude Law   2- Emma Watson
3- Stephen Fry   4- Morse
5- Inspector Lestrade

1- The lead detective in 'Prime Suspect' is Inspector Jane Tennison. Who played her?

A. Frances Barber

B. Pauline Collins

C. Julie Waters

D. Helen Mirren

2- Chief Wexford is a fictional detective working in the small town of Kingsmarkham in Sussex. Which writer created him?

A. Colin Dexter

B. Ruth Rendell

C. Agatha Christie

D. Leslie Charteris

3- In which city in England did Inspector Thursday work?

A. London

B. Birmingham

C. Manchester

D. Oxford

4- In which period are the stories about Inspector Foyle set?

A. The Second World War

B. The Cold War

C. The First World War

D. The Crimean War

5- Who plays Detective Chief Inspector Vera Stanhope?

A. Pam Ferris

B. Brenda Blethyn

C. Pauline Quirke

D. Linda Bassett

Answer

1- Helen Mirren   2- Ruth Rendell
3- Oxford   4- The Second World War
5- Brenda Blethyn

British Television:

1- Which is the longest running soap opera in England?

A. Eastenders

B. Casualty

C. Z Cars

D. Coronation Street

2- Who wrote "Only Fools and Horses"?

A. Tony Warren

B. John Sullivan

C. JK Rowling

D. William Shakespeare

3- What was "Emmerdale" originally called?

A. Down on the Farm

B. Emmerdale Manor

C. The Woolpack

D. Emmerdale Farm

4- Who was the first man to appear on Channel 4?

A. Jonathon Ross

B. Richard Whiteley

C. Stephen Fry

D. Lionel Blair

5- Which sitcom in the early 80s did Dame Judi Dench star in with her late husband Michael Williams?

A. Yes Minister

B. Me and My Girl

C. A Fine Romance

D. As Time Goes By

Answer

**1- Coronation Street   2- John Sullivan
3- Emmerdale Farm   4- Richard Whiteley
5- A Fine Romance**

British Television:

1- Who was the lead man in the sitcoms, "Man About the House", "Robin's Nest" and "Me and My Girl"?
A. David Jason
B. Richard O'Sullivan
C. John Thaw
D. Rod Hull

2- Who was the first host of "Top of the Pops"?
A. Jimmy Savile
B. Dave Lee Travis
C. Tony Blackburn
D. Noel Edmonds

3- What was unusual about the way Adam serenaded Rachel in the pilot of "Cold Feet"?
A. He was dressed as a Jester
B. He was playing the guitar
C. He was naked with a rose coming out of his bum
D. He was miming to 'Do You Love Me?'

4- Which of the actors who appeared in the first episode of "Casualty" remained in the cast the longest?
A. Derek Thompson
B. Maxwell Caulfield
C. Brenda Fricker
D. Cathy Shipton

5- First broadcast in March 2011, the television series 'Monroe' starred which actor in the title role?
A. Hermione Norris
B. James Nesbitt
C. John Thomson
D. Robert Bathurst

Answer
1- Richard O'Sullivan   2- Jimmy Savile
3- "C"   4- Derek Thompson
5- James Nesbitt

1- Which roller coaster has got four interversions, is the same as Nemesis and is at Thorpe Park?

A. Rush
B. Nemesis Inferno
C. Detonator
D. Colossus

2- Which ride in 1999 was Europe's tallest roller coaster, is 235 feet high and is at Blackpool Pleasure Beach?

A. Pepsi Max - The Big One
B. Big Dipper
C. Avalance
D. Zipper Dipper

3- Which roller coaster has ten inversions, and is at Thorpe Park?

A. Detonator
B. Slammer
C. Colossus
D. There isn't a 10 looper at Thorpe Park

4- Which roller coaster hangs for three seconds over the edge of the drop, is very close to another ride and is at Alton Towers?

A. Sky Swat
B. Enterprise
C. Batman the Escape
D. Oblivion

5- Which ride is a kids ride, has little hops and is at Blackpool Pleasure Beach

A. Spin Doctor
B. Bling
C. Zipper Dipper
D. Pepsi Max

Answer

**1- Nemesis Inferno   2- Pepsi Max - The Big One
3- Colossus   4- Oblivion
5- Zipper Dipper**

1- Which was the first British film to win the best picture at the Academy Awards?
A. The Deer Hunter
B. Oliver!
C. Tom Jones
D. Hamlet

2- Rachel Weisz won an Academy Award for Best Supporting Actress in which 2003 film based on a John le Carre thriller?
A. The Spy Who Came in from the Cold
B. Tinker Tailor Soldier Spy
C. Smiley's People
D. The Constant Gardener

3- "The Imitation Game" was a 2014 film based on which World War 2 Enigma machine code breaker?
A. Wallace Akers
B. Alan Turing
C. Edward Spears
D. Barnes Wallis

4- What part of London is 'Absolutely Fabulous' set?
A. East Dulwich
B. Westminster
C. Holland Park
D. Croydon

5- What series featured Dougal, Brian and Zebedee?
A. The Magic Roundabout
B. Mr Benn
C. Bagpuss
D. Newsnight

Answer
1- Hamlet (1948)   2- The Constant Gardener
3- Alan Turing 4- Holland Park
5- The Magic Roundabout

1- What programme had a prize of a Cheque book and pen?
A. The Prize is Right
B. Blankety Blank
C. University Challenge
D. Mastermind

2- What learning programmes are associated with bad knitwear?
A. History Programmes
B. Computer Programmes
C. Open University
D. Science Programmes

3- Which 'Good Life' performer spent most of their life in India?
A. Paul Eddington
B. Richard Briers
C. Penelope Keith
D. Felicity Kendall

4- Which of the programmes had special guests on their Christmas Special?
A. Morecambe and Wise
B. The Snowman
C. Dad's Army
D. Hancock's Half Hour

5- What was the first programme on Channel 4?
A. Friends
B. Countdown
C. Channel 4 News
D. Father Ted

Answer

1- Blankety Blank   2- Open University
3- Felicity Kendall   4- Morecambe and Wise
5- Countdown

1- "Are you sitting comfortably? Then I shall begin."
Which radio show used this catch phrase?
A. Andy Pandy
B. Storytime
C. Listen With Mother
D. Blue Peter

2- "How tickled I am." Which beloved Knotty Ash comedian uttered these immortal words?
A. Ken Dodd
B. Eric Morcambe
C. Ernie Wise
D. Jimmy Tarbuck

3- "Evening All". This short phrase was uttered by a uniformed constable. Who was he?
A. Allen of Ash Grove
B. Charles of Cutlers Close
C. Dixon of Dock Green
D. Badger of Broadmoor

4- "Ying tong iddle I po" was the catch phrase of Neddy Seagoon. Who played Neddy Seagoon?
A. Peter Sellars
B. Harry Secombe
C. Spike Milligan
D. Michael Bentine

5- Which London wide boy had the catch phrase "Lovely Jubbly"?
A. Rodney
B. Trigger
C. Del Boy
D. Boycie

Answer
1- Listen With Mother   2- Ken Dodd
3- Dixon of Dock Green   4- Harry Secombe
5- Del Boy

Bonus

1: Who was the UK Prime Minister between 1976 to 1979?
A. Margaret Thatcher
B. Edward Heath
C. James Callaghan
D. Harold Wilson

2: On 1 March 1946, what happened to the Bank of England?
A. Went broke
B. Went off the Gold Standard
C. Was robbed
D. Was nationalised

3: 'Money is like muck, not good except it be...' what?
(Francis Bacon - 1561-1626)
A. saved
B. wasted
C. spent
D. spread

4: Which type of ice-cream suggested the name of a 1987 TV series about a pop-group?
A. Strawberry Sundae
B. Tutti-frutti
C. Banana Split
D. Strawberry Sundae

5: Who founded Singapore and the London Zoo, but wasn't a gentleman thief?
A. Sir Stamford Raffles
B. Marco Polo
C. Sir Andrew Aguecheek
D. Lord Barnstaple

Answer

1: James Callaghan   2: Was nationalised
3: spread   4: Tutti-frutti
5: Sir Stamford Raffles

1: What type of dog is a cross between a greyhound and a collie?
A. Lurcher
B. Wazzock
C. Tripehound
D. Whippet

2: Derbyshire wryneck now known as goitre/goiter is an enlargement of which gland?
A. Lymph
B. Pituitary
C. Thyroid
D. Adrenal

3: Who was the first man to swim the English Channel without artificial aids, in 1875?
A. Lieutenant James Alkcock
B. Corporal John Pargeter
C. Captain Louis Bleriot
D. Captain Matthew Webb

4: Tarzan's 'real' name was John Clayton, but what was his title?
A. Lord Greystoke
B. Lord Sandwich
C. Lord Speke
D. Lord Clayton

5: What would you most likely be doing on a visit to Lords, The Oval, or Headingley?
A. Visiting royalty
B. Admiring works of art
C. Watching a cricket match
D. Answering to a judge

Answer

1: Lurcher   2: Thyroid
3: Captain Matthew Webb   4: Lord Greystoke
5: Watching a cricket match

1: What would the end of your email address look like, if you studied at a UK university?

A. .co.uk

B. .un.uk

C. .ac.uk

D. .ed.uk

2: London was the first city to host the Olympic Games on three occasions. In which years did it do so?

A. 1918, 1938, 2012

B. 1908, 1948, 2012

C. 1918, 1948, 2012

D. 1918, 1948, 2008

3: What connects English footballer Gary Lineker and Queen bassist John Deacon?

A. Both born in Leicester

B. Both born prematurely

C. Both born in 1955

D. Both born on a bus

4: The Falklands War was fought against which country?

A. Australia

B. Austria

C. Argentina

D. Albania

5: In the 1980s, if you asked, "Can I have a pee, please, Bob?" What were you most likely doing?

A. Asking to be granted entry to the toilet at a theme park

B. A contestant on the quiz show "Blockbusters"

C. Claiming a free gift at a fast food restaurant

D. Playing a prank on your school teacher

Answer

1: .ac.uk   2: 1908, 1948, 2012
3: Both born in Leicester   4: Argentina
5: A contestant on the quiz show "Blockbusters"

1: Who was Lord Haw Haw?

A. William Doyce
B. William Joyce
C. William Boyce
D. William Royce

2: In what game could you be LBW?

A. Rugby
B. Golf
C. Cricket
D. Tennis

3: Who was George Blake who escaped from prison in 1967?

A. A spy
B. A prison warder
C. A train robber
D. A murderer

4: Where would you find the oldest surviving clock in Britain?

A. Glastonbury
B. Salisbury Cathedral
C. Westminster Abbey
D. York Minster

5: In which year were identity cards abolished in Britain?

A. 1942
B. 1952
C. 1962
D. 1972

Answer

1: William Joyce   2: Cricket
3: A spy   4: Salisbury Cathedral
5: 1952

1: What in London was inaugurated by the Queen in 1984?
A. The Thames barrier
B. Canary wharf
C. The London eye
D. The Channel tunnel

2: Who, in September 1896, became the then-longest reigning monarch of England?
A. Henry VIII
B. Richard I
C. Elizabeth I
D. Victoria

3: What is the highest point in the British Isles?
A. Scafell Pike
B. Big Ben
C. Ben Nevis
D. Snowdon

4: Which famous building in London was historically used to house important political prisoners?
A. The Arsenal
B. Tower of London
C. The Royal Dungeons
D. Westminster Abbey

5: What is the capital of Wales?
A. Swansea
B. Aberystwyth
C. Cardiff
D. Ebbw Vale

Answer
1: The Thames barrier   2: Victoria
3: Ben Nevis   4: Tower of London
5: Cardiff

Printed in Great Britain
by Amazon

10229678R00061